Rich Couple$

GETTING BACK TO
FINANCIAL BASICS

Rich Couple$

GETTING BACK TO FINANCIAL BASICS

Evaluate and Manage Your Financial Means with a Cash Management Plan

JASON B. LEWIS

authorHOUSE®

AuthorHouse™
1663 Liberty Drive
Bloomington, IN 47403
www.authorhouse.com
Phone: 1-800-839-8640

Published by AuthorHouse   08/29/2012

ISBN: 978-1-4772-6605-2 (sc)
ISBN: 978-1-4772-6604-5 (e)

Library of Congress Control Number: 2012916119

To my wonderful wife Deserra, who always promised to walk hand-in-hand, beside me through life's journeys.

No matter what troubles have crossed our path; she has always ensured that it has been our path, together.

Thank you, honey

I love you.

"Before anything else, preparation is the key to success."

Alexander Graham Bell

CONTENTS

FOREWORD
By
Deserra D. Lewis

It is with a great sense of pride and appreciation that I write this 'foreward' introducing readers to Jason Lewis's book, "Rich Couples Getting Back to Financial Basics." This well-written, easy to follow book offers its readers a way to develop a written cash flow plan designed to help them evaluate their financial means and start living the life of their dreams. Jason has many professional contacts in which are all more knowledgeable in the area of financial education than I am. However, I am quite certain that his decision to choose me to write this important component was to extend the reality and everyday application of his teachings to his audience. Who better to write the 'foreward' of a book about couples getting back to financial basics than the wife of the author? My viewpoint will offer you a simple explanation of the book with the hopes that you are better able to relate to the principles being explained throughout.

You may be wondering what sets this book apart from the thousands of other books on finance and financial education. Furthermore, you may be wondering why even read and apply the ideas that are in this book to your life when you have so many other options. Both are very valid questions. I would say that the answer is simple. Take a look at what you have been doing in life financially and the position you are at this very moment. Are you where you want to be? Chances are that you aren't if you picked up a copy of this book. I have done my share of reading many books that fall within the category of finance and financial education, however, the simplistic approach this book takes will amaze you. For the most part, we all have the same goal of living our lives as happily and free as possible. This book will offer the tools you need in order to achieve that lifestyle.

Jason's immense passion for sharing his knowledge of financial education with others shines through in this book. He has developed a fool proof, and perhaps more importantly, a simple plan that is to be followed in order to ensure its success. Numerous seminars, readings, and correspondence with other financial professionals qualify him to write on such a popular topic. His plan includes six very basic steps that when followed, help couples start achieving their dreams. The book is broken down into chapters that offer explanation and applicable tasks for each action step. Furthermore, the book offers its readers visual aids and forms that will ultimately help simplify the process even more.

In the first chapter of the book, action above knowledge is described as the "golden nugget" to one's financial freedom. It astounds me that such a simple word like 'action' can create so much hesitation and fear in so many. The reality though is that it does, which is why I would say that this type of a challenging, yet non-threatening system is long overdue. This chapter continues as it offers readers a way to understand how to use the book and where to begin. It also gives a brief overview of what is to come later in the book. As you continue through the book, the format remains simple. An action step is given, fully explained, and then you are asked to complete an action task. References to important forms, which are provided in the appendix, are even provided to help guide you along. It can't get any more straightforward than that.

This book offers encouragement to its readers and challenges them to challenge themselves. It is relevant to everyone's life when you really stop and think about it. Look at the financial situation of our country in comparison to other countries in the world. Although, a much grander scale, this example illustrates how proper management or mismanagement of money can have drastic consequences. Only you have the ability to change your life financially and waiting too long to make that change can have devastating effects on your quality of life. The change starts here, with this book, so take action!

PREFACE

MY STORY . . .

The start to my financial education journey began with a very expensive mistake and four years of trying to make ends meet before I started to take planning my financial future seriously. I had always assumed that I would work for the military my whole life until I was eligible for retirement and figured I would let the military take care of me for the rest of my life.

However, while working at Home Depot between deployments in July of 2006, someone approached me and gave me a Robert Kiyosaki CD. That CD would be my first step towards finding my financial freedom. It would also start my six year self development and financial education journey.

The problem after six years was that I was not making any noticeable progress and getting very frustrated. I felt like the larger military leadership roles that I was taking on while serving in Iraq and Afghanistan were diverting my focus; little did I know that this was the furthest thing from the truth. My military service and larger military leadership roles were shaping me to become a better leader, mentor and financial educator.

I am proud of my military service; I took an Armor platoon of 16 and a Calvary troop of 90 men into a "war zone" and brought each one back alive. It was also an eye opening experience and I quickly learned how to manage a team, find and develop the strengths of each individual, and place them in the best positions to ensure overall mission accomplishment. It also taught me how to work with senior ranking officers from other countries as well as religious leaders and local nationals. Qualities I am now using to build my current financial education business.

You might think those six years of so-so results left me with negative feelings and thoughts or a sense of hopelessness. Well they didn't and in reality they taught me more about leadership, people skills, mind-set and money than I ever thought possible.

Let me now insert the fact that in six months after saving about $40,000 from my first military deployment, I not so successfully spent approximately $30,000 with nothing to show for it. When you blow $30,000 in six month—you are in desperate need of some financial education.

It was clear, what I didn't know about money was hurting me. If I was ever going to rise above "average," it was time for me to find and utilize some serious financial education strategies and knowledge. It was time to break the cycle of poor money management and start to act, think, and create the habits of the rich. Wasting away $30,000 was a bitter pill to swallow, but I chose to look at it like a $30,000 lesson.

The next step toward my goal of financial freedom was to start a Cashflow 101 Club and network with others who were interested in increasing their financial education and expanding their financial context. It was important to me to find others who were like minded, tired of living pay check to pay check and who wanted financial freedom for their family.

In case you do not know, the "Cashflow 101 Board Game" was created by Robert Kiyosaki in order to teach financial education in a fun, simple way. If you have not played the game, I recommend you do so. To be honest, I knew very little about what to do—I had only played the Cashflow 101 game a few times but starting a Cashflow Club felt like the right thing to do. I learn better by doing; taking action, if you will. What I didn't know was that I would find ways to make extra money while I strengthened my financial background and helped others. I also found ways to have my money to work for me.

The club helped me begin meeting and networking with other leaders and I made contact with many entrepreneurs and successful individuals in the northern Georgia area! Here's the best part—I discovered the "key" to creating financial freedom; you need to have a system. When you have the right system you don't need to stress about what to do, because the system guides you through that process. All you need to do is be willing to take action and hold yourself personally responsible for your success or failure.

Once I realized that systems were the way to create massive success for people, my focus shifted from just playing Cashflow 101 on a weekly basis with a few people to creating a system that would do four things for those who were willing to follow it:

1. Teach couples how to manage their financial means.
2. Teach couples how to increase their financial education.
3. Teach couples how to increase their financial means with the four asset classes.
4. Teach couples how to protect their financial means and create legacy income.

Finding out about systems helped me enter a whole new world of financial education and entrepreneurship. I learned that if I truly wanted to succeed in life that I needed to begin teaching what I knew to other people; provide the most value for them that I could. It became very important to me to help people plug into the right system, work with the right team, have access to the latest cutting-edge education, leaders and mentors.

What I now need are a few good motivated men and women, who are ready to take their lives and income to a new level. I fully understand that not everyone is ready to jump into this thing called financial freedom. Although, if not now, WHEN? Remember, 6 years and a $30,000 mistake is how I started my journey.

This life change will take a commitment of time, money and the desire to invest in your most important asset, which is YOU. Even if you are a complete newbie, you will able to step into this system and start using it right away. I know this because I have seen it work. The more problems that I solve for people and the more hurdles I am able to clear away help me provide the most value.

In this day and age, you get ahead by helping those within your network and when its time they will lift you up. However just know that I alone will not be able to carry you past the finish line of success—you will need to step up and do your part. But I will not leave you behind, if you're willing to put in the effort.

The Truth About Financial Education

The truth is if you do not have financial education, any type of investing is "RISKY!" In a time where there is uncertainty and fear around money, the economy, and job security—financial education is more important than ever.

Financial Education has become more than just a subject of interest, it has become my business. No I am not Robert Kiyosaki or Dave Ramsey; I do not live off my passive income and speak to thousands of people (yet). I am simply an individual who made the decision to take control of my life, my finances and my business. When I did, the perfect opportunities opened their doors.

You may not think you have what it takes (right now) to better manage your financial means and increase your financial education and that's okay because with a system you have a team, a stable base from which to learn and grow.

So, the only way you're going to know if you have what it takes is by continuing to read. Information is free and it never hurts to learn something new. After your done reading, you will know if you are ready to advance your life and income to the next level. See you on the other side.

Jason Lewis

ACKNOWLEDGEMENTS

Writing this book was somewhat stressful but mostly a freeing experience. It was freeing because when you have lived as much of this material as we have and experienced success with these concepts, it feels amazing to know now others will experience the same success in their lives. I wish to thank all those people who have inspired me through the task of writing this first book:

To my friends and mentors, thank you for being my editors, readers and examples of how couples are supposed to conduct themselves relationally and financially.

To my mother, whose entrepreneurial spirit has always told me to get up and go on.

To my Lord Jesus, for the guidance and direction You have provided me while writing this book, for the many blessings You have bestowed upon my family, and for Your grace without which I would be lost.

INTRODUCTION

Do What the Rich Do

If you are reading this book then chances are you have reached a crossroad in your life where you are trying to figure out what you need to do financially. You are to the point where you feel like you have read one too many books but think maybe if I read one more; I will get that one golden nugget I need. You think maybe this book will give you that one answer that you have been looking for.

If I described you above and you are hoping this book will give you that one secret, then let me be very clear before you read any further. This book's secret, this books golden nugget is simple:

> *In order to be successful with your finances you must take ACTION. Your success and financial freedom has less to do with how smart you are or how much information you have and more to do with the ACTIONS you take to implement the information you have gathered or been given.*

In this book you will learned to change the way you thinking about money and expand your financial context. You will open yourself up to a new and exciting path of opportunity. You will also learn the basics of financial literacy and how to use that knowledge to take action. Remember knowledge builds confidence, and confidence leads to action.

CHAPTER 1

BEGINNING TO EVALUATE YOUR FINANCIAL MEANS: THE BASICS

So you have made the choice to seek financial freedom. You have sought the financial education that will help you on your path. Now let's move forward and begin creating the foundation for your financial plan.

Over the past 6 years during my search for financial freedom, I have said myself or heard others say, "If only I had started focusing on my finances sooner, things would be different" or "If I only knew then what I know now, I would not be in debt and I would have more assets." I have also been asked many times, "What should I do in order to get my personal finances together?"

When people first started asking me that question, I have to be honest; I wasn't quite sure what to tell them. However, now that some time has passed and I personally have taken some ACTION, I feel as though I am now qualified to give an answer to the question, and to be honest the answer is quite simple. What I mean to say is that the answer is simple, but what people struggle with is not the answer. The desire to learn, and more importantly, the desire to take action, is what people struggle with.

The reason I say this is because we live in the information age, so lack of answers is not a problem. Finding answers to pretty much anything is easy; you just have to "GOOGLE" it. What to do with those Google search results is what makes people scratch their heads and fail to take action.

So what I am going to do over the course of the following pages is to answer the question: "What should I do in order to get my personal finances together?"

However, before I answer that question, I want to be very straightforward with you. I find that it is important to only work with people who truly want what I have to offer—who truly want to LEARN.

That being said, I would only recommend that you continue past this point under three conditions:

1. You really want to learn.
2. You understand there is no secret formula, no magic pill.
3. Information alone is useless—You must take ACTION, in order to be successful.

That being said let the process begin!

How to Use This Book and Where to Begin

The best way to achieve success with this book is to apply what you have learned to build a solid foundation and begin building wealth. If you do this, you will be doing what the rich DO.

So what will follow in this book is a hands-on, step-by-step approach that is designed to help set up your financial defense by first helping you increase your money management skills and learn how to "work" your money.

This book will cover the six basic Rich COUPLE$ Action Steps and will help get you headed in the right direction financially:

Step 1—Acknowledge Your Regret, Then Destroy It.
Step 2—Determine Your Values and Assess Your Options.
Step 3—Set Goals: Determine where you want to be financially.
Step 4—Get Organized.
Step 5—Determine Your "Cash Management Plan."

Step 6—Implement Your "Cash Management Plan."

You will begin this process by first acknowledging your regret—and then destroying it. You will do this because it signifies a mental shift in your mind from being a victim to being the masters of your life. Once you have made this decision and you are able to take control of your financial situation. You can begin to take action and be proactive instead of simply reactive.

After acknowledging you regret you will determine what is important to both you and your spouse by determining your values; then figure out if you are really living within your values. This step may seem out of place but knowing how you spend your time and your money is a direct reflection of what you see as important in your life. Many people cannot acknowledge this fact but you will need to do so in order to define and set your financial goals.

After determining your values and assessing your options, you will set new and exciting goals, get organized and determine your financial plan. These last three ACTION steps will help you defend your bottom line. When you begin to take control, manage your cashflow and learn to "work" your money you will then be ready to use your mind and money to invest in your family's financial future.

As you read and work through these pages, you will find it extremely helpful to take action and apply the information covered in each section. Highlight sections and take notes on pointers that are especially relevant to your situation. Go at your own pace. And most importantly, do not give up.

Whenever fear or doubt block your path, circle around these obstacles and continue on. You will find that with every ACTION step you take, your confidence grows—along with your cashflow and assets. Remember, the reward is not only the freedom that money buys, but also the confidence you gain in yourself—for they are really one in the same.

CHAPTER 2

STEP 1—ACKNOWLEDGE YOUR REGRET, THEN DESTROY IT

> "We all make mistakes, have struggles, and even regret things in our past. But you are not your mistakes, you are not your struggles, and you are here NOW with the power to shape your day and your future."
>
> **—Steve Maraboli**

Some of you place 100 percent blame on yourself for your current financial station in life and to an extent I can understand where you are coming from. However, I also know that many of you are in your current financial situation not because you were careless, negligent, or irresponsible, but because somewhere along the way life threw you a curve ball. Either way the past is the past, what's done is done and now it is time to get down to business because you cannot go back and change what has already happened.

Now in order to get started, there are two things in this step that you must do, the first is "identify and acknowledge your regret," and the second is to "destroy that regret." You must be willing to do both before you can move on to Action Step 2, which is "Determine Your Values and Assess Your Options." The reason you must complete Action Step 1 first is because until you can move past your regret, pain, and thoughts of your past failures you cannot look toward the future and determine what your options are to create success in your life.

Acknowledgement of Your Regret

Acknowledgement is the first step because it signifies a mental shift from being a victim to becoming the master of your life. This step also gives you complete control over your destiny. Once you've made the decision that you are going to take control of your financial situation, you've made the decision to take action; to be proactive instead of simply reactive.

Through acknowledgement, you can begin the process of taking back control over your finances as well as begin to master your thoughts and your actions. Until you take control it is useless to move on to any of the other steps in this book, simply because lack of control will result in failed efforts and results. Once you have acknowledged that your financial situation is not where you want it to be, then it is time to forgive yourself.

Up to this point in your life, you did the best you could with the information you had. Forgive yourself for letting the past happen the way it did, for not doing what you knew was smart fiscally, or for what you could have done. Whatever happened happened and you cannot change the past; you can only become stronger from it.

My guess is most if not all of you, who are reading this book have been doing this for years if not decades. It is unreal how tough we are on ourselves, but I can tell you from experience that I was one of the worst offenders. I am my own worst critic and if you do not believe me ask my wife! If I had to guess, I'd say you are your own worst critic too.

That being said, I may not know you individually or be able to tell you what has happened in your past that is still affecting your quality of life. Only you know if it was something you did, or failed to do. If it was something someone else did or did not do. You may even be feeling regret as a result of a major, devastating event-such as a bitter divorce, having had to declare bankruptcy, or going through a humiliating public disgrace. Your regret may stem from a cluster of minor setbacks. Whatever the cause, regret can be incredibly toxic and it must be removed from your life if you want to move forward.

Fortunately, there are ways to overcome regret, and even benefit from it. Neal Roese, Ph.D., is one of the top scientists at the Kellogg

School of Management, who studies regret. He's the author of *If Only: How to Turn Regret into Opportunity*. Roese explains that regret has a good side. The human brain is predisposed to look for ways in which we could have done things differently or gotten a better result, not to make us feel bad, but in order to help us improve.

So in a sense, the real purpose of regret is to help us make better decisions in the future, and to get us to modify our behavior in order to get better results. As of today you need to start looking at regret as a signal that leads you to ask yourself questions such as the following:

1. How can I prevent this from happening again in the future?
2. What do I need to do differently in the future to make sure that, next time, I get what I want?
3. What can I learn from this?
4. If you could go back and coach yourself through what happened, what advice would you give yourself?
5. What behavior modification is necessary?

Destroy it—Releasing Your Regret and Getting on with Your Life

Once you have taken the time and honestly thought about and answered the questions above, it is time to complete your first **action task.** I read about this action task in the book *Start Late, Finish Rich—A No-Fail Plan for Achieving Financial Freedom at Any Age*, by David Bach. David calls this, "the fastest way to let it go." So here it is, utilize the Rich COUPLE$ Releasing Your Regret form, Form #1 in the appendix of this book or get yourself a blank sheet of paper and write down a list of as many of your personal "if only's" you can think of. Your "if onlys" could be things like:

1. If only I had saved more money.
2. If only I had not taken the job I have.
3. If only I'd had kids.
4. If only I had not bet on the Atlanta Braves
5. If only I had not put that trip to the Bahamas on my credit card.

They don't have to be only financially related, since you are taking the time to do this, you might as well get rid of any and all of those things you have been beating yourself up about all these years.

Now, when you are finished making your list . . . . Destroy It!!! That's right I am serious destroy it by any means necessary. Burn it! Rip it up! Or flush it! Let all of those "if only's" go.

Once you have destroyed your list, you should feel better. You should understand now that the past is the past and that it is now time to look towards your future. You are now prepared to move to Action Step 2—Determining Your Values and Assessing Your Options. Good Luck!!

CHAPTER 3

STEP 2—DETERMINE YOUR VALUES AND ASSESS YOUR OPTIONS

> "Your beliefs become your thoughts, your thoughts become your words, your words become your actions, your actions become your habits, your habits become your values, your values become your destiny."
>
> **—Mahatma Gandhi**

This step may seem a little out of place for financial planning. Most people ask me, "What do my values have to do with my finances?" I say to them, "Stop for a minute and think about it, is there anything more important than your values?" All of your decisions are based on your own personal set of values. What you drive; where you travel or live; how much of your money you spend, save or invest; or what you focus your time and energy on—are all affected by your values.

This is why after my wife and I had successfully completed Action Step 1; we could with 100 percent certainty generate a clearer picture in our minds of what we valued most in our life. The past didn't matter anymore we were only focused on the present and more importantly the future. This helped us to understand why we had had experienced success with our joint finances and why so many others had failed miserably managing their joint finances. We were better able to figure out how to create our personal financial plan and now so can you.

So What's Really Important to You?

At this point you need to complete an **action task**. Both you and your spouse need to take about 30 minutes on your own to write down what your top five values are.

Remember, we are talking about values not goals. Values are security, happiness, freedom. Goals are paying off your mortgage, getting debt free, buying a boat, going on a vacation.

This may be a tough exercise if you have never really thought about it before, so if 30 minutes is not enough time to get the job done right, then take an hour or two. However, ensure that both you and your spouse commit to getting back together in a certain timeframe (1-2 days) to discuss and agree not to move on to any other action steps until this one is complete.

Constructing Your Values Wheel

Ok, now that you both have taken the time to figure out what your strongest values are, it's time to talk to each other about those values. This experience can be and is very eye opening for many couples because this may truly be the first time ever, both of you will have to express to each other what's really important to you.

Also use this time to really discuss and figure out if your actions and financial choices currently line up with your values. Many times people will realize that what they choose to spend their money on has nothing to do with what's important to them but has everything to do with what's important to their family, friends, or society.

We all, myself included, spend so much time trying to have and do more, that we never look up to see whether who we are is who we want to be. To put it another way, this process is basically a matter of getting to the root of what is most important to you, and then planning your finances around that.

Once you both feel confident that you have expressed yourself, it is time for your second **action task**. Write your values down on a Values Wheel. Utilize the Rich COUPLE$ Values Wheel form, Form # 2 in the appendix of this book.

The Value Wheel serves a few purposes, the first being that it forces you to write your values down and things that are written down are prioritized higher and focused on more often than things that are not. Second, the values wheel helps people see that they need to have balance amongst their values, so imaging that your values are similar to the spokes of a wheel can help. This is significant because if the spokes on a wheel are different lengths, meaning more value is placed on certain ones over others then the wheel will not roll, ultimately preventing us from reaching our goals.

Bringing It All Together

This process may seem simple, but don't be fooled. It can also be very powerful. Indeed, within weeks after you complete this exercise you will most likely be much further along with your financial plan than you have been in the past few years.

This is because now not only do you better understand what's important to you but also what's important to your spouse. The ability to see through the clutter allows you to communicate more efficiently, which increases the desire to want to achieve commons goals. Money is great to have, but all the money in the world won't make you happy if what you do with it conflicts with your own or your family's values.

CHAPTER 4

Step 3—Set Goals: Determine Where You Want to be Financially

"People with goals succeed because they know where they are going."

—Earl Nightingale

Now that you and your spouse have a better understanding of what you both value most in life and have started to communicate consistently about it. It is time to discuss setting some joint and personal goals, based on these values.

For example, if you chose, security as one of your top values, then one of your financial goals could be on a specific date to, start putting aside 10 percent of your income for your families emergency fund. Another example could be if you chose excitement as one of your top values, you could on a specific date, start putting aside $50 a week to eventually take your family on small monthly trips to exciting places around the country.

The bottom line is that goal setting is a powerful process that helps focus your thinking about your ideal future. It can also motivate you to turn your vision of your ideal future into reality. So by knowing precisely what you want to achieve, you will be better able to concentrate your efforts. You will also be able to quickly spot the distractions that can, so easily, lead you astray. Whatever you want to do that is in line with your values needs to be considered. Do your best to really think about and examine what you want, leave no thought or idea out of the conversation.

As you discuss and begin to really think about what you want; start to create a list of all your ideas. Why do you need to write them down? Because, athletes, successful business-people, lawyers, doctors, and great achievers in all fields use written goal setting techniques. Statistics show people who write down their goals have over an 80 percent higher success rate of achieving them. Short-term goals are usually simpler and easier than long-term goals.

So why is writing down your goals so important? Well, writing them down can help you build momentum, resulting in more frequent victories. Because when you do this you experience more excitement and motivation as you work towards achieving those goals you may have thought were impossible. Also remember as you start to reach those goals, reward yourself for achieving them.

To get you off to a good start you need to complete an **action task**. Using the Rich COUPLE$ Goal Setting form, Form #3 in the appendix of this book. Take your five "values" and write down three to five goals for each value that you believe would help you live out that value.

So as an example, if one of your values was security, then your list of three to five goals with your value would look something like this:

Security: (Big Picture)

1. Have $50,000 in my emergency fund
2. Invest in assets for retirement
3. Increase my income
4. Start my own business

Now that you have an example, it's your turn to write down your top five values and their corresponding goals. Remember, this process may take some time. Resist the urge to rush through this step because this is the foundation and starting point for all of your future success. Utilize the Rich COUPLE$ Goal Setting form, Form #3 in the appendix of this book.

If you are having trouble figuring out how to construct your goals, first focus on your "big picture," those large-scale goals that you want to achieve. What do you want to do within this value say over the next 10 years? Once you figure out what your "big picture" goals are, it is time to break them down into smaller targets, targets that you will need to complete in order to reach each of your large-scale goals. As you do this, you will want to make sure that each of your goals are SMART. SMART stands for: specific, measurable, achievable, results-oriented, and timely.

The creation of the SMART goals acronym is highly debated and some say that potentially Steven Covey, Paul J. Meyer, W. Edwards Deming, George T. Doran or George Odiorne can be credited with its creation. However, I would say that the true origins here are of little importance. We should focus on what happens when you plan your steps wisely by setting SMART goals. The time you take now to establish well thought out goals will be what allows you to create future success in your life.

SMART Goals

S—Specific: Goals should be straight forward and emphasize what you want to happen. A specific goal has a much greater chance of being accomplished than a general goal. Specifics help (you) focus your efforts and clearly define what you are trying to do. Specifics are the What, Why, and How of the SMART model.

Ensure the goals you set are very specific, clear, and easy to understand. Instead of setting a goal to just get out of debt, set a goal to pay off your debt that has the lowest payoff balance first; by putting all of your extra income aside to pay it off quicker. Then once that loan is paid off, you can focus on the next loan/debt.

M—Measurable: If you can't measure it, you can't manage it. There are usually several short-term or small measurements that can be built into the goal.

Choose a goal with measurable progress so you can see the change occur. How will you know when you've reach your goal? Establish concrete criteria for measuring progress towards the attainment of each goal you set. Be specific! "I want to pay off my $1,000 loan within 10 months" shows the specific target to be measured. "I want to pay off my car loan" is not as measurable. To determine if your goal is measurable, ask questions such as . . . . How much? How many? How will I know when it is accomplished?

When you measure your progress, you stay on track, reach your target dates, and experience the exhilaration of achievement that spurs you to continue to apply the effort and motivation required to reach more goals.

A—Attainable: When you identify goals that are most important to you, you begin to figure out ways you can make them come true. You develop the attitudes, abilities, skills and financial capacity to reach them. Your begin seeing previously overlooked opportunities to bring yourself closer to the achievement of your goals.

Goals you set that are too far out of reach most likely won't be achieved. You can attain any goal you set when you plan your steps wisely and establish a time frame that allows you to carry out those steps. Goals that may have seemed far away and out of reach eventually move closer and become attainable, not because your goals shrink, but because you grow and expand to match them. When you list your goals you build your self-image. You see yourself as worthy of these goals, and develop the traits and personality that allow you to possess them.

For instance, aiming to pay off a $1,000 loan in one week isn't attainable. But setting a goal to pay $100 per month over 10 months is. And once you have achieved that aiming to roll that $100 over to your next debt also becomes attainable. The success you gain from this momentum will help you to remain motivated.

R—Realistic: This is not a synonym for "easy." Realistic, in this case, means "do-able." It means that the skills needed to do the work are available; that the project fits with the overall strategy and goals of your family. A realistic project may push your skills and knowledge, but it shouldn't break them.

Devise a plan or a way of getting to your goal which makes that goal realistic. The goal needs to be realistic for you and where you are at the moment. A goal of never again using a credit card to pay for things may not be realistic. However, it may be more realistic to set a goal of ensuring you put aside the amount you want to charge in an account so that you can pay it off without a penalty when your statement is due.

Be sure to set goals that you can attain with some effort! Too difficult and you set the stage for failure, but goals that are too easy send the message that you aren't very capable. **Set the bar high enough for a satisfying achievement!**

T—Timely: Set a timeframe for the goal: for next week, in three months, or five years. Putting an end point on your goal gives you a clear target to work towards.

If you don't set a timeframe, the commitment is too vague. It tends not to happen because you feel you can start at any time. Without a time limit, there's no urgency to start taking action now. Timely also means the timeframe must also be measurable, attainable, and realistic.

SMART goals are important and effective but I like to add two additional qualities to the SMART goals model, making them SMARTER Goals. The E stands for "evaluate regularly" and the R stands for "repeat daily". I like these additions. They are good reminders that goals must constantly be evaluated and possibly changed or updated, as well as repeated to keep them in the forefront of our minds. Stale goals lose their relevance. Goals that are no longer relevant should be changed, shelved or eliminated. Below are the two additional qualities that will make your goals SMART-ER.

E—Evaluated Regularly: Achieving your goals means having a plan because without one, success is very unlikely and as Harvey McKay said, "Failures don't plan to fail; they fail to plan." Sometimes you'll notice that your plan is only yielding small results or results that are not what you had in mind. Only by evaluating your plan, goals and the steps you're taking to get where you want to go, will you have a chance to succeed. Evaluation is a worthwhile activity because it can help keep you honest about your efforts, it can also reveal holes in your plan and it can inspire you to keep going when you notice even moderate results happening in your favor. Commit to evaluating your goals on a regular basis to ensure you achieve marked success in all areas of your life.

R—Repeat Daily: Put your goals in a place that can be seen on a daily basis. Read your goals out loud in the morning and at night. Repeat your goals in your head throughout the day whenever you can. Write your goals daily to reinforce them or carry them on a laminated card in your wallet or purse. The benefits of repeating your goals will not be immediately recognizable but rest assured the seeds you have been sowing will bear fruit over time.

Remember to always utilize the SMART goal model whenever you set your goals because everyone can and will benefit from goals and objectives that are SMART-ER.

CHAPTER 5

STEP 4—GET ORGANIZED

"An idea can only become a reality once it is broken down into organized, actionable elements."

—Scott Belsky

I can tell you that it was very important for you to figure out what your values and goals were because they will become your solid foundation. You can also always look at them when times get tough during the journey ahead to give you some motivation and perspective to keep you on track. Now that you have a better understanding of what you value and have set your financial goals, it's time to focus on your actual financial situation.

Getting organized sounds harder than it is, especially when it comes to your personal finances. Remember, that the hardest part is actually getting the courage to look at the mess you have made or perceived to have made. Really after you understand what you are working with, you may find that it's not as bad as you previously thought it was. It's not to say that you will like what you see but at least you now know the road ahead of you.

The best way to get a handle on your total financial situation is to first create a system for filing and keeping all your personal financial documents in order and accessible. This will help you by allowing you to organize everything so you can easily find and reference it as needed.

I recommend using a hanging file folder system. All you need to set this up is a hanging file folder box, crate or cabinet, about 15 hanging files and 100 manila folders. The most important items that you will need to track are: Taxes (7 years back), Retirement Accounts, Social Security Documents, Investment Accounts, Savings and Checking Accounts, Household Accounts, Credit Card Debts, Other Liabilities (debts other than credit cards and mortgage) and Insurance. These nine accounts are the most important and will help you have a better understanding of your total financial situation.

At this point you need to complete the first **action task** of Step 4: Create your filing system so that you can store, access and understand your personal financial documents. Utilize the Rich COUPLE$ Financial Freedom File Folder System form, Form #4 in the appendix of this book to get you started. You can modify the system as needed but these documents should give you a good base.

Realistically this task should not take you very long, maybe 2-4 hours. Although, to ensure you do it properly set aside some time and put it on your calendar to get this done. The reason I say plan it and put it on your calendar is so that both you and your spouse can participate. Both parties need to feel they are an active participant of this process.

Once you have completed your file folder system its then time to move to the second **action task** which is filling out your the Rich COUPLE$ Financial Inventory Worksheet form, Form #5 in the appendix of this book. All you really need to do for this task is take the inventory worksheet sit next to your file folder system and fill the worksheet out. Each folder in your file system should have all the information you need to fill in each question or blank within the inventory.

The Rich COUPLE$ Financial Inventory Worksheet is broken down into the following section:

Section 1: Family Information
Section 2: Personal Investments
Section 3: Retirement Accounts
Section 4: Real Estate
Section 5: Estate Planning

Section 6: Income Sources
Section 7: Expenses

Important note: Remember that this sheet is for your reference and to help you gain a better understanding of your current financial situation. However, this sheet should be locked in a secure location as it has all of your personal identifiable information, which could be used by someone to take over your life potentially in a negative way.

Once you have finished putting together your file folder system and filled in the Financial Inventory Worksheet you are now prepared to move to Step 5: Determine Your "Cash Management Plan."

CHAPTER 6

STEP 5—DETERMINE YOUR CASH MANAGEMENT PLAN

"The first step to getting the things you want out of life is this: decide what you want."

—Ben Stein

So, now that you have an accurate picture of your overall values, goals and financial situation. It is time to be brutally honest with yourself and decide whether you and your spouse think you are on the right track or if you need to overhaul your current financial plan.

I would say that my guess is if you have read to this point in the book, that you are like approximately 80 to 90 percent of American households who operate without a detailed; accurate financial plan. If this is you then my guess is that you both have decided that a total financial overhaul is needed. This overhaul needs to start in the form of a cash management plan.

Don't get discouraged, because cash management planning is not as painful as most people make it out to be. Something to make this easier for you is as you go through this process think of yourself as a small business. The reason I say think of yourself as a business is because what would you say the chances of success are for a business that keeps no records and has no plan to forecast its income or expenses? You would probably say the chances for failure are very high and the chances for any type of measureable success are almost nonexistent.

To use an expression that I used earlier in this book: When we fail to plan, we plan to fail. Without a plan you will consistently feel like there is always too much month left at the end of the money.

Determining Your Plan

Determining your written cash management plan is really just a matter of deciding what your priorities are and then communicating on paper where you both want your money to go. Notice I said, written plan. I say this because having a written cash management plan is absolutely necessary. It is necessary to take the scattered financial information in your brain, categorize it, and then summarize. Having a written plan has the similar benefits that having written goals have.

The first and most immediate benefit from having a written cash management plan is being able to easily find answers to those financial questions that have been stumping you for so long. The second benefit to having a written cash management plan is the new financial clarity you will experience and the ability to see a light at the end of the debt and financial problems tunnel.

Now that you understand the importance of a written cash management plan it is time for you to complete some **actions tasks**. In this next section I will present four specific tasks that you need to follow in order to develop the most effective written cash management plan possible.

Action Task #1 Determine Your Spending Habits: Track Your Spending.

Determining your spending habits is important because you and your spouse have established financial habits that you may not even be aware of and those habits may sabotage your attempts at putting together an accurate written plan. Not to mention, if you are in a bad financial situation, tracking your spending will also give you an idea of where your money goes and how much money you spend.

What you need to do is, first, go and get a notebook, financial ledger or use the example Rich COUPLE$ Track Your Spending form, Form #6 in the appendix of this book and for the next 30-60 days write down every purchase you make. If you do this properly and stick to it at the end of 60 days you will have written proof and a better idea of where you money goes and how you spend it. This will prove beneficial later as you execute Action Task #4 Commit to Your Plan for Ninety Days.

Action Task #2 Stop Accumulating Unnecessary Debt and Curb Your Spending.

This action task is probably the toughest of the four action tasks because you must face the grim reality of how much you owe and who you owe it to. It is easy to lie to yourself and pretend you are ok, which is what many people do, but fighting that temptation, holding yourself accountable and facing the hard facts is the best thing for you, your spouse and your family.

Will Rogers a comedian and humorist has a saying that goes, "When you've found that you've dug yourself into a hole . . . . Stop digging." You basically need to put a freeze on all debt, stop adding to your existing credit card balances or adding new loans. Start ensuring you pay off whatever you charge the month you purchase it, curb your spending or stop using your credit cards all together. This task alone will force you to be much more cognizant of what money is flowing out.

Action Task #3 Write Out the Details of Your Written Cash Management Plan

In Step 4, Get Organized you filled out the Financial Inventory Worksheet and that worksheet will now help you to lay out your monthly cash management plan. If you didn't take the time to fill out this worksheet, do so now. This worksheet will help you gain clarity and more control to help ensure that you are better off than a large majority of couples in America today.

In reference to the Rich COUPLE$ Financial Inventory Worksheet, I want to take a moment to point out what I feel are the two most important sections of that document.

Section 6 the **Income Sources** section of the inventory. This section will help you figure out how much your making and from what quadrant that income is coming from. If you are not sure what I mean by *quadrant*, then I suggest you read the book *Cash Flow Quadrant: Rich Dad's Guide to Financial Freedom,* by Robert Kiyosaki. In this book Robert lays out the four primary ways in which people earn money. The four ways are employee, the self-employed, big business owners, and investors. Knowing where your income is generated from and being able to chart a course from where you are to where you want to be in the future is very important.

Section 7 the **Expenses / Debt** section of the inventory. This section will helps you prioritize and ensure you're considering any and all expenses and debts you have in your life. Currently the expense and debt categories are prioritized in the order that Dave Ramsey outlines in his New York Times bestselling book, *Financial Peace Revisited.*

1.   Paying Yourself First (Saving, Tithing and Investing)
2.   The Four Walls (Home, Utilities, Food, and Transportation)
3.   Everything Else (Clothing, Medical, Personal, Recreation and Debts)

This is also the same order that my wife and I prioritize our expense and debt categories. However, I suggest that you prioritize these categories however you and your spouse like because this is ultimately your cash management plan and it has to work for your family.

One category that you might need an explanation for is the "Blow" category. This is also a concept from Dave Ramsey's book. He says you need to plan to blow, waste, or not account for some portion of your money. If you do not plan this, you will always do it anyway. The problem is that most of us have this category now. The problem really is that most couples blow category is their entire plan. A regimented plan that is too strict is not realistic. If you do not allow some wiggle room in your plan, it and ultimately you will fail.

Always remember that a good plan lives and moves—it is dynamic and changes as your life changes. It may take you three to four months or even more to flush out your plan. Initially you might have to review your plan four to five times a month and make adjustments. You may have budgeted too little for some areas and too much in others.

Just remember that this will be a little frustrating, but that is because you have lived on an ill-prepared budget or no budget for a long time. It will take you a few months to get your plan to be realistic for your lifestyle.

The purpose of the cash management plan is not to complicate your life but to simplify it. Once you begin to realize where your money is and what you are spending it on life gets easier to manage.

Action Task #4 Commit to Your Plan for Ninety Days

For most of you committing to following your cashflow plan for ninety days might seem like forever, but remember you have tried living your life with no plan for about 20 to 30 years, maybe even longer. That means you have lived without a plan for that long and look at where it has gotten you. I would say in most cases it has not gotten you to where you were hoping to be by this point in your life.

So why not give these suggestions a real opportunity to take hold. A one-month trial run and the, this is too hard I can't do this attitude, isn't a fair analysis. I am not asking you to commit to this for me, but for you and your family. Commit to the full ninety days and I mean really commit.

When you commit, you are committing to not let anything pull you away. If you do not set out with a firm commitment, you will give up within the first three weeks or maybe even sooner. If you will stay with the ninety days, however, I promise that you will work the kinks out and your financial life will never be the same. Turn to the appendix of this book to read and sign the Rich COUPLE$ 90-day Cash Management Plan Commitment Letter, Form #7.

Remember this, that ninety days is less than 1 percent of your lifetime, and if you have read this far, you have what it takes to do it.

CHAPTER 7

Step 6—Implement Your Cash Management Plan

"If you do the things you need to do when you need to do them, then someday you can do the things you want to do when you want to do them."

—Zig Ziglar

Congratulations you've just committed to sticking to your Cash Management Plan for 90-days and now that you have reached the last chapter of this book—Implement Your Cash Management Plan, it can be easy to feel a bit overwhelmed by everything. You might even be saying to yourself, "Ok but now what do I do, how do I implement this plan?"

What I want you to remember as we move forward, is that "success in life comes one day at a time," or as Jeff Olson suggests in his book *The Slight Edge*, one step at a time. This chapter will show you how to use the cash management plan that you and your spouse have put together to make those daily financial decisions that will be the ultimate key to your financial success.

Keeping it Simple

To better illustrate my point that the best way to achieve financial success occurs one step at a time, I want to retell a story from the Georgia backwoods that a friend of mine told me. There once was a strong young man who was known far and wide as the strongest man in the county. One day he was challenged at the county fair to a test of strength by a very thin old man. The old man bet that he could break a bundle of sticks in half and that the strong young man couldn't.

The cocky young man accepted the bet. So a choice number of sticks were tightly bundled and the contest began. The poor young man was sweating, bruising his knee, and making himself miserable, but alas was unable to break the sticks. The old man stood slowly, stretched a little, walked over to the bundle, untied it, and broke the sticks one at a time with ease. The old man and his wisdom were the talk of the county fair. That is how you work towards having a great financial situation, one stick (or step) at a time.

The Priority of Actions Steps

From my experience working with couples I have found that the best way to begin moving towards your financial success is not by only breaking the process down into action steps, but also prioritizing them. That said my guess is that the order of implementation is what you are after—how to prioritize the process.

Below is the process to work through with extra money, bonus money, and money from selling unwanted items, gifts, or even extra cash found in your monthly budget. Use this money to attack each step of your cash management plan. Do not however, cash in retirement plans early to get out of debt or to use in this process; the penalties and taxes will be terrible and ultimately hurt you in the long run. However, you should temporarily stop adding to your retirement plans or investments until you've reached the correct action step.

Cash Management Plan (Action Steps)

1. Emergency Fund ($500 to $2,000)
2. Debt Reduction Planning.
3. Emergency Fund Plus (3-6 months expenses)
4. Invest in Assets (4 asset classes)
5. Save for College
6. Give

Action Step #1 (Emergency Fund)

Plan into your budget to pay the minimum on everything, you will use the excess money from your budget once everything is paid to put towards your goal of $500 to $2,000 in savings. In addition to the excess money from your budget, you should figure out other ways to generate extra money. This is so you can complete this action step as quickly as possible. This emergency fund is your first level of protection in case something happens. Having this money put aside will protect you from little emergencies. I can tell you from experience that once my wife and I had our first $1,000 in our emergency fund we stopped experiencing emergencies. And so far we have never had to use our emergency fund. I think it is because we always plan for things or figure out how to adjust our budget so that we don't have to use our emergency fund.

Action Step #2 (Debt Reduction Plan)

It is now time to attack your existing debt. Implement your Debt Reduction Plan and pay off all personal debts except your home mortgage. Attack your debts with vigor and throw whatever you can at them.

The next question you may have is which debt do we start with? Many experts advise paying your high interest debts off first. Obviously, this makes the most sense mathematically. But if money were all about math, you wouldn't have debt in the first place. Debt is as much about emotion and psychology as it is about math. There are many approaches to debt reduction but the one that I recommend is using what Dave Ramsey calls a *Debt Snowball*. The debt snowball offers big payoffs, payoffs that can speed up the debt reduction process. Utilize the Rich COUPLE$ Debt Reduction Planner, Form #8 in the appendix of this book. Here's the short version of how the *Debt Snowball* works:

1. List your debts from lowest balance to highest.
2. Pay the minimum payment on all debts *except* for the one with the lowest balance.
3. Throw every other penny you possibly can at the debt with the lowest balance.

4. When that debt is gone, do not alter the monthly amount used to pay debts, but throw all you can at the debt with the next-lowest balance.

My wife and I love the debt snowball. Until we discovered it, we thought we'd never get out of debt. Though it still takes time to pay off your debts, you begin to see results almost immediately.

Action Step #3 (Emergency Fund Plus)

At this point the only debt you should have left is your house mortgage. It should be relatively easy now to save the rest of your emergency fund. Now just like there are multiple ways to reduce your debt, there are also many opinions about how much to put aside for your emergency fund. The conventional wisdom is to have enough set aside to cover three—to six-months' worth of living expenses.

From my experience working with couples who are just starting this process, this is an attainable goal. However, for each couple the fully funded emergency fund amount will vary; some couples may need a larger cushion to feel like they have enough saved for a rainy day and some less. Whatever the amount you decide on, remember to keep this money liquid but not easily accessible. The best way is to keep your emergency fund in a simple money market or bank savings account that gives you the ability to have checks. I want to make sure to point out that you do not invest with this money. It is only for the purpose to protect you from the unexpected.

Action Step #4 (Invest in Assets)

This step is important because it begins to build upon the strong foundation you have laid for your family by creating and implementing your cash management plan. At this point, you must realize that if you want to become rich and secure your family's financial future, you have to do what the rich do with their money which is investing it in assets. Assets are investments that put money in the income column on your financial statement. Investing of any kind can seem overwhelming but just as with any new skill, profitable investing takes time and a commitment to learning or getting educated.

Investing not only requires financial education but also capital. Since most people usually don't have the amount of capital required to become an investor right away, the first thing you need to do is start by putting a percentage of your gross household income aside. You need to do this while you are getting educated in your investment(s) of choice. Putting aside this income is to help you save the appropriate amount of capital to begin investing in one or many of the four asset classes that you choose.

My recommendation is after you fully fund your emergency fund to begin by putting aside 15 percent of your gross household income in a money market or bank savings account. This should give you a great start and give you the capital you will use to invest in your first couple of assets, at least until your assets begin generating income for you. Then over time as your assets begin to generate income for you, you will then take that income and reinvest it into purchasing more assets. The assets you choose will be based on your investment strategy and plan you and your spouse have put together. This practice is what will help increasing your portfolio and the amount of cash flowing into the income column of your financial statement. Then once your assets begin generating cashflow for you, you can take the 15 percent of your gross household income and put it towards other goals or dreams.

If you are not sure, the four asset classes are businesses, real estate, paper assets (stocks, bonds, mutual funds), and commodities. From my own experience I recommend that you first look into owning your own business. This may seem like a bold statement however, owning a business is one of the best ways to create an ongoing residual income. A business that you can see an immediate return on your investment, will become a valuable asset for you and your family. Then once you begin to generate income from your business you can then take that income and purchase other assets, which will increase your portfolio and passive income. So if owning a business is something that peaks your interest, before you jump in with both feet, I recommend that you read, *The Business of the 21ˢᵗ Century* by Robert T. Kiyosaki. This book should give you a great idea of the different types of businesses that are available. It will also give you insight to the business that Robert Kiyosaki, Donald Trump and Warren Buffet think is the best business for the average person.

Outside of my recommendation to begin investing in assets by starting your own business, I want to say that it is really up to you which assets you chose to invest in. I say this because you need to ensure that you know as much as you can about each investment before you begin investing in it. I am a strong believer in financial education, as it is the single most important form of knowledge you can have that directly affects your quality of life, and the quality of life of those who depend on your income. Financial education empowers you to be the best that you can be and helps you to think "outside the box" that so many of us are confined by. I challenge you to learn something new, make a change in your life and start acting like the rich by investing in the four asset classes.

Action Step #5 (College Savings)

For most of us, the thought of choosing ourselves at the expense of our children is pretty hard to imagine. However, now and only now is it time for you to start saving for your children's college fund. You feel guilty—I know but don't you dare do college funding until you get the first four steps of this process completed. Many experts liken it to those flight safety announcements. You are supposed to put your own oxygen mask on first before you help your child with theirs, no matter how counterintuitive that might feel as a parent. I know those little blue eyes make your blood run cold when you know that the college fund isn't there, but the only way to build a strong house is to lay the proper foundation first, and guilt is not a building block. Just let those brown eyes be a motivator to help you run—I mean, sprint—to this step.

If you took the time and really focused on action steps one thru four by setting the proper foundation then you are in a great position and have some options to save for your children's college. The fact is that there are multiple options for funding your children's college however; you need to be willing to use your financial intelligence instead of working hard to achieve the goal of funding your child's college education. The best advice I can give you is understand all your options before selecting the one(s) that are right for your family.

Action Step #6 (Give)

This is the part I enjoy the most about the Rich COUPLE$ Strategy—getting rich so that you can give. Giving is an important part of being successful and financially free. The act of giving induces feelings of abundance and those feeling of abundance draw more success and financial freedom to your door step. With no more debts and a great cash management plan in place, there is nothing left to do but continue to build wealth through assets and give some of it away. As discussed earlier in *Action Step Four* by using the four asset classes, you are now the rich getting richer. When opportunities to invest in deals such as the $100,000 deal that can be bought for $50,000 present themselves, you will be there with cash in hand adding to your assets column, which increases your cashflow as well as increases your ability to give to those in need. Welcome Aboard.

Now that you better understand the Action Steps to implementing your cash management plan. What will you do? Will you try to cheat and sidestep any of the steps? I hope not because the penalty in the financial game for cheating is stepping back two steps for every step sidestep you decide to take. All broke people think there are short cuts, and the rich, who remain rich know differently.

CHAPTER 8

CLOSING—JUST DO IT

"Opportunity is missed by most people because it is dressed
in overalls and looks like work."

—Thomas Edison

This book has focused on something that few American households
have done or will ever do, namely executed the six Rich COUPLE$
Action Steps listed in the beginning of this book, which walk you
through how to create a written cash flow plan. This written plan
then will help you evaluate your financial means, get you back on track
financially and eventually help you create the life of your dreams.

I cannot stress enough the importance of this process as a method
for evaluating your financial means in order to help get you back on
track. A written cash management plan does not have to become a chore
in your mind nor does it have to become overwhelming. I have worked
with so many couples on the brink of financial disaster, and it makes
me sick inside when I know that a simple, written cash management
plan could have saved most of them numerous heartaches, a lot of
money and sometimes their relationships.

Give this six step process a chance, commit to completing each of
the action tasks and seeing this process through and I know you will
be on your way to evaluating and managing your means in order to
eventually increase them.

APPENDICES

FORM 1

---⊶⊷⊶---

RELEASING YOUR REGRET

Utilize this form to list as many of your personal "If only's" you can think of. They don't need to all be financially related. Since you are doing this, you might as well get rid of any and all things you have been beating yourself up about all these years. If you have more than 15 "If only's" then use a blank sheet of paper and continue.

1. _____
2. _____
3. _____
4. _____
5. _____
6. _____
7. _____
8. _____
9. _____
10. _____
11. _____
12. _____
13. _____
14. _____
15. _____

Now that you are finished making your list . . . . Destroy it! Destroy it by any means necessary. Burn It! Rip It Up! Shred It! Or Flush It! Finally let all of those "If only's" go.

FORM 2

Values Wheel

The Value Wheel serves a few purposes, the first being that it forces you to write your values down and things that are written down are prioritized higher and focused on more often than things that are not. Second, the values wheel helps people see that they need to have balance amongst their values, so imaging that your values are similar to the spokes of a wheel can help. This is significant because if the spokes on a wheel are different lengths, meaning more value is placed on certain ones over others then the wheel will not roll, ultimately preventing us from reaching our goals.

See the Values Wheel below, fill in your top 5 values, in the boxes provided.

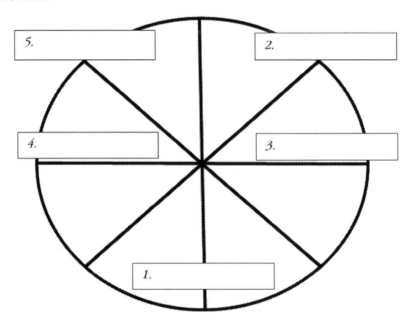

FORM 3

GOAL SETTING FORM

Use this Goal Setting Form to capture, in writing your top 5 values and their corresponding goals. Prior to filling out this form you need take some time and figure out what your "Big Picture" goals are for each value and then select 3-5 "Shorter Term" goals that will help you achieve your "Big Picture" goal. Remember this is an important part of your financial planning. These values, big picture and short term goals will lay the foundation for what you want to achieve financially for you and your family. Take this seriously and you will be pleasantly surprised by the results.

Value #1: _____

Big Picture Goal: _____

_____

Sub-Goal 1: _____

Sub-Goal 2: _____

Sub-Goal 3: _____

Sub-Goal 4: _____

Sub-Goal 5: _____

Value #2: _____

Big Picture Goal: _____

_____

Sub-Goal 1: _____

Sub-Goal 2: _____

Sub-Goal 3: _____

Sub-Goal 4: _____

Sub-Goal 5: _____

Value #3: _____

Big Picture Goal: _____

_____

Sub-Goal 1: _____

Sub-Goal 2: _____

Sub-Goal 3: _____

Sub-Goal 4: _____

Sub-Goal 5: _____

Value #4: _____

Big Picture Goal: _____

_____

Sub-Goal 1: _____

Sub-Goal 2: _____

Sub-Goal 3: _____

Sub-Goal 4: _____

Sub-Goal 5: _____

Value #5: _____

Big Picture Goal: _____

_____

Sub-Goal 1: _____

Sub-Goal 2: _____

Sub-Goal 3: _____

Sub-Goal 4: _____

Sub-Goal 5: _____

FORM 4

—⊗⊗⊗—

FINANCIAL FREEDOM FILE FOLDER SYSTEM

This simple file folder system will allow you to <u>organize</u> your financial documents so that you can <u>easily access</u> them for reference purposes. The idea and concept for this system can from a book I read called *Start Over, Finish Rich,* written by David Bach. When your financial documents are <u>neat, in order,</u> and you can easily find them you will be more likely to use them. By using the documents that you receive every month you can gain a better understanding of your current financial situation.

In order to make this work you will have to make a commitment to yourself and your significant other to get this done. Do not put this off, do this exercise while it is still fresh in your mind. This system can also be used with other more well known money management systems such as Quicken, QuickBooks, Mint.com, etc.

So here is what I want you to do. First, I want you to get yourself a dozen hanging folders and a box of at least 50 file folders to put inside them. Then using a pen or marker <u>label the hanging folders</u> with the numbered headings below.

1. TAX RETURNS: In this hanging folder, put eight file folders, one for each of the last seven years plus one for this year. Place a label on each of the eight folders and write in the last two digits of the year (i.e. TAX RETURN FOR YEAR: 20*10*). Put into each folder that year's important tax documents, such as W-2 forms, 1099's, and a copy of all the tax returns you filed. If you failed to keep these documents but used a professional tax preparer in the past, call him or her and ask for back copies. If you didn't use a professional tax preparer then I would recommend in the future investing in one so you don't waste

the time and energy you could be using on something else on this time consuming task. Let the people who went to school for tax preparation, make it easy for you. As a rule, you should keep your old tax records for at least seven years because that is how far back the law allows the IRS to go when it wants to audit you.

2.   RETIREMENTS ACCOUNTS: In this hanging folder, put a file folder for each of your retirement accounts. Place a label on the folder and fill it out (i.e. Account Holders Name: *John Doe*, Account Name: *XYZ*, Account Type: *401(K)*). The most important thing to keep in these folders is the accounts <u>quarterly statements</u>. You don't need to keep the prospectuses that the mutual-fund companies mail you each quarter. However, if you have a company retirement account, you should definitely keep the sign-up package because it tells you what investment options you have—something you should review annually. If you don't have this sign-up package anymore then get a hold or your benefits contact at the company where you work and get another one. I recommend that you also sit down with this person quarterly and find out what changes have been made or future changes that will affect your account in the future.

3.   SOCIAL SECURITY: In this hanging folder, put a file folder for your most recent Social Security Benefits Statement. Place a label on the folder and fill it out (i.e. Name on Statement: *John Doe*, SSN Last 4: *1234*). If you haven't received one in the mail, get online and go to *www.ssa.gov* to request one. If you don't have internet access, telephone your local social security office (the number is listed on the front of most phone books under "Federal Government).

4.   INVESTMENT ACCOUNTS: In this hanging folder, put a file folder for each of the investment accounts that you have. Place a label on the folder and fill it out (i.e. Account Holders Name: *John Doe*, Account Name: *USAA*, Account Type: *Asset Management*, Account Number: *1234567890*). If you own mutual funds, maintain a brokerage account, or own individuals stocks, each and every statement you receive that is related to these investments should go in a particular folder.

5. SAVINGS AND CHECKING ACCOUNTS: In this hanging folder, put a file folder for each checking and savings account that you have. Place a label on the folder and fill it out (i.e. Account Holders Name: *John Doe*, Bank Name: *Bank of America*, Account Type: *Checking*, Account Number: *1234567890*). Keep your Savings and Checking monthly statements here.

6. HOUSEHOLD ACCOUNTS: In this hanging folder, have a file folder for each document that has to do with your home. Place a label on the folder and fill it out (i.e. House Title, Home Improvements, etc). The folder House Title should contain your title information (if you can't find this information, call your real estate agent or title company). The folder Home Improvements is where you will keep all the receipts for any home-improvement work you do (since home-improvement expenses can be added to the cost basis of your house when you sell it, you should keep these receipts for as long as you own your house). The folder Home Mortgage will contain all your mortgage statements (which you should check regularly).

If you are a renter, this folder should contain your lease, the receipt for your security deposit, and the receipts for your rental payments.

7. CREDIT CARD <u>DEBT</u>: In this hanging folder, have a file folder for each credit card account that you have. Place a label on the folder and fill it out (i.e. Account Holders Name:_*John Doe*, Company Name: *Visa*, Card Type: <u>Personal, Business</u>). However many files you have keep all of your monthly statements in them. And hang on to them. As with tax returns, I would keep all my credit-card records for at least seven years in case the IRS ever decided to audit me.

8. OTHER LIABILITIES: In this hanging folder, have file folders for each debt you have other than your mortgage and your credit-card accounts. Place a label on the folder and fill it out. These would include college loans, car loans, personal loans, etc. Each debt should have its own file, should contain the loan note and your payment records.

9. INSURANCE: In this hanging folder, have a file folder for each of your insurance policies, including health, life, car, homeowners

or renters, disability, long-term care etc. Place a label on the folder and fill it out (i.e. Company Name: *Humana*, Policy #: *12345678*). In these folders put the appropriate policy and all the related payment records.

10. FAMILY WILL or TRUST: In this hanging folder, have a file folder for each will or living trust, along with the business card of the attorney who set it up.

11. CHILDREN'S ACCOUNTS: In this hanging folder, have a file folder for all statements and other records pertaining to college savings accounts or other investments that you have made for your kids. Place a label on the folder and fill it out.

12. FINANCIAL FREEDOM INVENTORY PLANNER: Finally, create a folder called the "Rich COUPLE$ Financial Inventory Worksheet." This is where you will keep your Financial Inventory Worksheet and a running semi-annual total of your net worth; a vital record that will help keep track of your net worth.

CONGRATULATIONS! If you have made it this far, then you have done more than 90% of the rest of the Americans in the United States. You should feel great about the progress you've made. Remember you did the hard part by actually taking the time to create this system. Now all you have to do is implement it. Just put the files together as best you can and simply make a note of what you don't have.

I recommend that you choose one day per week and make it your financial clean up day. Use an hour or two on the chosen day to work on filling one of the folders and talking about or study the documents you put into it. This might do more for you than you think. One of the things that keeps people from moving forward with their financial freedom is that they are afraid to think or speak about their current financial situation. This act of filling one folder per week and talking about it might just be what you need to move forward and create success in your life.

**USE-Avery 5266 Filing Labels, to print and use for your hanging and file folder.

FORM 5

FINANCIAL INVENTORY WORKSHEET

SECTION ONE: FAMILY INFORMATION

Full Name: _____ Date of Birth: _____
Age: _____

Spouse's Name: _____ Date of Birth: _____
Age: _____

Mailing Address: _____
City: _____ State: _____ Zip: _____

Marital Status: Single:_____ Married: _____ Divorced: _____ Other:

Home Phone#: _____
Cell Phone#: _____ Spouse's Cell#: _____

Employer: _____ Job Tile: _____
Work Phone#: _____ Fax: _____

Spouse's Employer: _____ Job Title: _____
Spouse's Work#: _____ Fax: _____

Email Address: _____
Spouse's Email: _____

SS#: _____ Spouse's SS#: _____

Are you retired?

Yes _____ Date Retired _____

No _____ Planned Retirement Date _____

Is your spouse retired?

Yes _____ Date Retired _____

No _____ Planned Retirement Date _____

CHILDREN

	Name	Date of Birth	SSN
1)	_____	_____	_____
2)	_____	_____	_____
3)	_____	_____	_____
4)	_____	_____	_____
5)	_____	_____	_____

DEPENDENTS

Do you have any family members that are financially dependent upon you or could be in the future? (i.e parents, grandparents, adult children, etc.)

Yes _____ No _____

	Name	Relationship	Age
1)	_____	_____	_____
2)	_____	_____	_____
3)	_____	_____	_____
4)	_____	_____	_____
5)	_____	_____	_____

SECTION TWO: PERSONAL INVESTMENTS

(Do not include retirement accounts here)

CASH RESERVES

List amount in Banks, Savings & Loans, and Credit Unions

	Bank	Type of Account	Interest Rate
1)			
2)			
3)			
4)			
5)			

FIXED INCOME

List fixed income investments: CD, Treasury Bills, Notes, Bonds, and Series EE Savings Bonds

	Investment Type	Amount	Current %	Maturity Date
1)				
2)				
3)				
4)				
5)				

STOCKS

List the stocks you own.

	Symbol	# Shares	Purchase $	Value	Purchase Date
1)					
2)					
3)					
4)					
5)					

**DO YOU HAVE STOCK CERTIFICATES IN A SECURITY DEPOSIT BOX? _____ YES _____ NO

MUTUAL FUND and/or BROKERAGE ACCOUNTS

	Firm Name	# Shares	Cost Basis	Value	Purchase Date
1)					
2)					
3)					
4)					
5)					

ANNUITIES

	Company	Owner	Interest Rate	Value	Purchase Date
1)					
2)					
3)					
4)					
5)					

OTHER ASSETS (Business ownership, etc.)

Asset Name	Asset Type	Value
1) _____	_____	_____
2) _____	_____	_____
3) _____	_____	_____
4) _____	_____	_____
5) _____	_____	_____

SECTION THREE: RETIREMENT ACCOUNTS

EMPLOYER SPONSORED

Are you participating in an Employer Sponsored Retirement Plan?

(These include Tax-Deferred Retirement Plans such as 401(k) Plans, 403(b) Plans and 457 Plans) _____YES _____ NO

YOU

Company	Plan Type	Value	% Contribution
1)			
2)			
3)			
4)			
5)			

SPOUSE

Company	Plan Type	Value	% Contribution
1)			
2)			
3)			
4)			
5)			

Do you have money sitting in a company plan you no longer work for?

YOU

_____ YES _____ NO BALANCE _____

When did you leave the company? _____

SPOUSE

_____ YES _____ NO BALANCE _____

When did you leave the company? _____

SELF-DIRECTED RETIREMENT PLANS

Are you participating in a Retirement Plan?

(These include IRA's, ROTH IRA's, SEP-IRA's, SAR-SEP IRA's and SIMPLE PLANS) _____YES _____ NO

YOU

	Company	Plan Type	Value	% Contribution
1)				
2)				
3)				
4)				
5)				

SPOUSE

	Company	Plan Type	Value	% Contribution
1)				
2)				
3)				
4)				
5)				

SECTION FOUR: REAL ESTATE

Do you rent or own your own home?

Own _____/Monthly Mortgage is _____
Rent _____/Monthly Rent is _____

Approx. Value of Primary Home $ _____
- Mortgage Balance $ _____
- Equity in Home $ _____
- Length of Loan _____
- Interest Rate of Loan _____ is loan <u>Fixed</u> or <u>Variable</u>

DO YOU OWN A SECOND HOME?

Approx. Value of Primary Home $ _____
- Mortgage Balance $ _____
- Equity in Home $ _____
- Length of Loan _____
- Interest Rate of Loan _____ is loan <u>Fixed</u> or <u>Variable</u>

ANY OTHER REAL ESTATE OWNED?

Approx. Value of Primary Home $ _____
- Mortgage Balance $ _____
- Equity in Home $ _____
- Length of Loan _____
- Interest Rate of Loan _____ is loan <u>Fixed</u> or <u>Variable</u>

SECTION FIVE: ESTATE PLANNING

Do you have a WILL or LIVING TRUST in place _____ YES _____ NO
Date it was last reviewed? _____
Who helped you create it? Attorney's Name

_____

Address _____
Phone Number _____ Fax _____
Is your home held in the trust or is it held in joint or community
property? _____

RISK MANAGEMENT / INSURANCE

Do you have a protection plan for your family? _____ YES _____ NO

Company	Type	Death Benefit	Value	Premium
1) _____	_____	_____	_____	_____
2) _____	_____	_____	_____	_____
3) _____	_____	_____	_____	_____
4) _____	_____	_____	_____	_____
5) _____	_____	_____	_____	_____

TAX PLANNING

Do you have taxes professionally prepared? _____ YES _____ NO
Name of Accountant / CPA _____
Address _____
Phone Number _____ Fax _____
What was your last year's taxable income?

_____

Estimated tax bracket? _____

SECTION SIX: INCOME SOURCES

Source	Amount (Dollar Value)	Period / Describe Bi-Monthly ($1^{st}/15^{th}$)
1) Salary 1		
2) Salary 2		
3) Salary 3		
4) Bonus		
5) Self-Employment		
6) Interest Income		
7) Dividend income		
8) Royalty Income		
9) Rents		
10) Notes		
11) Alimony		
12) Child Support		
13) Unemployment		
14) Social Security		
15) Pension		
16) Annuity		
17) Disability Income		
18) Cash gifts		
19) Trust fund		
20) Other		
21) Other		
22) Other		
23) Other		
24) Other		
25) Other		

SECTION SEVEN: EXPENSES (FIXED / VARIABLE) AND DEBT

(Listed in Order of Importance)

Item	Sub Total	Total

1) **Giving**
   a. Tithing _____
   b. Charity _____ _____
2) **Saving**
   a. Emergency fund (1) _____
   b. Retirement Fund _____ _____
   c. College fund _____ _____
3) **Housing**
   a. First Mortgage _____
   b. Second Mortgage _____
   c. Homeowners Insurance _____
   d. Repairs / Maintenance _____
   e. Home Furnishings _____ _____
4) **UTILITIES**
   a. Electricity _____
   b. Water _____
   c. Gas _____
   d. Phone _____
   e. Cable _____
   f. Internet _____
   g. Trash _____ _____
5) ***FOOD**
   a. Grocery _____
   b. Restaurants _____
   c. Fast food _____
   d. Other _____
   e. Other _____ _____
6) **TRANSPORTATION**
   a. Car Payment (1) _____
   b. Car Payment (2) _____
   c. Gas and Oil _____
   d. Repairs / Maintenance _____

    e. Car Insurance   _____
    f. License/Tags/Taxes   _____
    g. Car Replacement   _____ _____

Item	Sub Total	Total

7) CLOTHING
    a. Children   _____
    b. Adults   _____
    c. Cleaning and Laundry   _____ _____

8) MEDICAL / HEALTH
    a. Disability Insurance   _____
    b. Health Insurance   _____
    c. Doctor   _____
    d. Dentist   _____
    e. Optometrist   _____
    f. Pharmacist   _____ _____

9) PERSONAL
    a. Life Insurance   _____
    b. Child Care   _____
    c. Baby-Sitter   _____
    d. Toiletries   _____
    e. Cosmetics   _____
    f. Hair Care   _____
    g. Education / Adult   _____
    h. School tuition   _____
    i. School Supplies   _____
    j. Child Support   _____
    k. Alimony   _____
    l. Subscriptions   _____
    m. Organization Dues   _____
    n. Gifts (Inc. X-Mas)   _____
    o. BLOW $$$ _____ _____

10) **RECREATION**

a.	Entertainment	_____
b.	Vacation	_____
c.	Airfare	_____
d.	Vehicle Rental	_____
e.	Other	_____
f.	Other	_____ _____

Item	**Sub Total**	**Total**

11) **DEBTS (Hopefully $0)**

a.	Credit Card (1)	_____
b.	Credit Card (2)	_____
c.	Credit Card (3)	_____
d.	Credit Card (4)	_____
e.	Credit Card (5)	_____
f.	Credit Card (6)	_____
g.	Gas Card (1)	_____
h.	Gas Card (2)	_____
i.	Dept Store Card (1)	_____
j.	Dept Store Card (2)	_____
k.	Finance Co. (1)	_____
l.	Finance Co. (2)	_____
m.	Credit Line	_____
n.	Student Loan (1)	_____
o.	Student Loan (2)	_____
p.	Other	_____
q.	Other	_____
r.	Other	_____
s.	Other	_____
t.	Other	_____ _____

FORM 6

———— ⚬⚬⚬ ————

TRACK YOUR SPENDING

Determining your spending habits is important because you and your spouse have established financial habits that you may not even be aware of and those habits may sabotage your attempts at putting together an accurate written plan. Not to mention, if you are in a bad financial situation, tracking your spending will also give you an idea of where your money goes and how much money you spend.

Item	Date	Total

So for the next 30-60 days write down every purchase you make. If you do this properly and stick to it at the end of 60 days you will have written proof and a better idea of where you money goes and how you spend it.

FORM 7

90-Day Cash Management Plan
Commitment Letter

I AM A PERSON OF ACTION WHO TAKES 100% RESPONSIBILITY FOR THE QUALITY OF MY LIFE.

FOR THE NEXT 90 DAYS _____ TO _____ I MAKE A SOLEMN PLEDGE TO MYSELF AND MY FAMILY TO FAITHFULLY COMMIT TO IMPLEMENTING THE CASH MANAGEMENT PLAN THAT MY SPOUSE AND I HAVE CREATED WITHOUT EXCUSES OR EXCEPTIONS

I AM NOW A MEMBER OF A UNIQUE CLUB COMPRISED OF THOSE WHO ARE TIRED OF THEIR CURRENT FINANCIAL SITUATION AND WHO HAVE VOWED TO CHANGE AND CHOOSE THEIR THOUGHTS AND ACTIONS ACCORDINGLY, TO ACHIEVE FINANCIAL FREEDOM IN OUR LIVES.

SIGNED ON THIS _____ DAY OF _____.

DAY   MONTH   YEAR

SIGNATURE:_____

FULL NAME:_____

WITNESS SIGNATURE: _____

WITNESS FULL NAME: _____

FORM 8

———— ⌘ ————

DEBT REDUCTION PLANNER

Debt is as much about emotion and psychology as it is about math. There are many approaches to debt reduction but the one that I recommend is using what Dave Ramsey calls a *Debt Snowball*. The debt snowball offers big payoffs, payoffs that can speed up the debt reduction process.

Here's the short version of how the *Debt Snowball* works:

1. List your debts from lowest balance to highest.
2. Pay the min. payment on all debts *except* for the one with the lowest balance.
3. Throw every other penny you possibly can at the debt with the lowest balance.
4. When that debt is gone, do not alter the monthly amount used to pay debts, but throw all you can at the debt with the next-lowest balance.

Remember to redo your Debt Reduction Plan each time you pay off a debt so you can see how close you are to getting out of debt.

Item	Total Payoff	Min. Pymt.	New Pymt.	Pymts Left

ABOUT THE AUTHOR

Jason Lewis graduated from North Georgia College and State University with a Bachelor's degree in Psychology and a Minor in Leadership. Upon graduation, he commissioned as an Officer into the Georgia Army National Guard where over the past eight years he has lead Soldiers while deployed to Iraq and Afghanistan. This is a significant part of his story because he had always assumed he'd work for the military until retirement. However, things have a way of changing and after a very expensive mistake upon returning from his first deployment; Jason began taking planning for his financial future seriously. What he didn't know about money became clear to him and he chose to break the cycle of poor money management and start to think and act like the wealthy.

Financial Education has become more than just a subject of interest for Jason . . . it has become his business. He simply made the decision to take control of his life, finances, and business. Once he did, the perfect opportunities opened their doors.

Now in his first book "Rich Couple$ Getting Back to Financial Basics," Jason imparts his hard-earned personal knowledge about finances in a straightforward, down-to-earth manner. Not an economics major, Jason is just your average Joe who wants to help others achieve their financial dreams.

Jason lives in Statesboro, GA with his amazing wife Deserra and they are expecting their first child Ryean Jean in September 2012. Jason would like to learn about your experiences using "Rich Couple$ Getting Back to Financial Basics." Please share with him at jason@yourstylenow.com.